AF251598

All
that
so
simple

# All that so simple

## Poems by Neil Myers

Purdue University Press
West Lafayette, Indiana
1980

Some poems in this volume, reprinted here with permission, have appeared in the following periodicals: *Abraxas* ("For My Father in Florida," "Summer Tune"); *The Antioch Review* ("Icarus, Shot for a Bird"); *Caterpillar* ("For Rachel," "War Poem, 1968"); *The Chariton Review* ("August, Late," "The Revolution Is Accomplished"); *Epoch* ("Apropos"); *Eros* ("Set Piece"); *High/Coo* ("Starling," "Field"); *The Hiram Poetry Review* ("Wrap Up"); *Indiana Indiana* ("Weather"); *Indiana Writes* ("All That, So Simple," "Country Journal"); *Kansas Quarterly* ("Late Report"); *Mississippi Valley Review* ("Anything You Want," "Ch'ad G'ad Yaw," "1972"); *On the Cusp* ("A Couple of Days"); *Perspective* ("1963: A Girl Abducted"); *Seer Ox* ("In Time," "The Willow Is Green, the Flower Red," pending); *Texas Quarterly* ("Three for My Father," pending). "Memory of Italy," "1913," and "Friday Nights" were originally published in *Esquire* magazine. "For Su Tung-P'o" was first published in *Mademoiselle*.

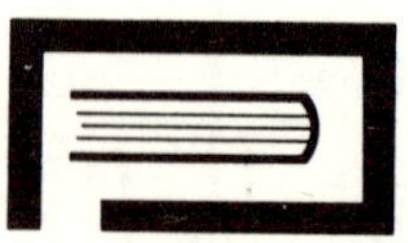



Library of Congress Catalog Card Number 78-71637
International Standard Book Number 0-911198-56-3
Printed in the United States of America

*For Lorna, Rachel, Julie,
and my mother and father.*

# Contents

# Acknowledgments

My gratitude to Hank Childers, Ellen Kennedy, Lee Perron, Don Seybold, and Felix Stefanile for their warm and persistent encouragement and advice. I also wish to thank the president and trustees of Purdue University for a sabbatical leave which enabled me to finish this book.

# ICARUS, SHOT FOR A BIRD

something of what he had been hearing
shot thru him savagely,
the weather with its autumn lies.
a casual scene

fell down below. a thing of air
escaped to its hole.
below, in the ditch, in the dull yards,
good old boys

their dumb red faces intact, watched him,
grinning, reddening,
a mile from their sullen shacks.
he was flying

but in a kind of wave, a movement
of different densities.
gravel rained, branches fell toward
him, seeds ripped

his hands, thorns groped in his body. this
was certain, & angry,
& apart. the light caught in the rims stood
savagely immense

& rocked the chaos of states: child, man, *that*.

## MICHELANGELO'S BUST OF
## BRUTUS IN THE BARGELLO

like a bunched fist, the colorations
& the knead, of marble,
a thing to stripe, attenuate,
in the palm of a hand that could never
lift or balance it alone

the face turns, the eye
has a cauliflower ear, the hair
hangs over like peach-colored fringe,
the mouth is a lined branch, the brow
a blank, the neck a trunk of
twisted, sputtering light

name it brutus, something
that had forgotten to stand up for other truth,
or never sat, or looked suddenly out at anger
like an assassin, made out of fruit
so ripe it would touch the earth
like a grenade
a hand's span off

*the man who moves toward action from a thought*

SET PIECE

always, at the first snow,
they go to the windows &
rub the glass with smilers
&, if it's deep enough, go

out & roll the clumsy molds
they call angels, waves of
torsos wing to wing, until
it's half a battlefield, tho

real angels are concrete &
these are hollow. who taught
you that, i ask, but they
don't know: no one, we just

lie down & shake. for days
i see their forms in fog &
milky air, open & cheap as
names on shirts & banks, &

heading for plain zero, hip
& thigh, tho maybe that's an
angel, indecently exposed &
out of tune with anything

we say: i & my village, yard
full of folk, the bears just
left this for you, shape-
less & cold, & danced away.

## "THE WILLOW IS GREEN,
## THE FLOWER RED"

sekiun's
poem
hanging on my
bulletin board
5 years

toward the right the
kanji
& next to them the
english

small faded handwriting
the paper is dirty
a torn strip with nearly invisible
blue lines up & down

    yanagi
    willow

    wa

    middori
    green

    hana
    flower

    wa

    kurenai
    red

the pain i feel
is purely my own

PROVINCETOWN, 1973:
READING AKHMATOVA

rain on the day-green, the statue at
the pond edge, its nose loose, its
pecker gone. the huge locust lifts
its swarthy leaves, the water urges
belches & debris, & i hear yester-
day's, "in russia . . . poets . . . last voic-
es of—" what? candor, void & fog?
*russia, idiot of the world* (carlos
williams, who wasn't dispossessed
but wanted more), mother of poets as
we mother junk & smog, is life simple
for you, will it disperse you? one
writes well near catastrophe, said
mandelstam, too close to lie easily.

# LATE REPORT

tonight, against the rain & anger
in our voices, they crowd us, giv-
ing us nothing to push back but our-
selves. later, we see the things

they have left out: a baby, a cut-
out groom & bride, a half-winged
butterfly being bottled to death,
that beats at the glass in air that

is just gas, until i take it to the
door & watch it in the streetlight
climb & fall. rain fills the pot-
holes in the alley where tomorrow

they can dig the stones all knuckle-
blank they treat as jewels. the news
tonight is two parts cruelty, one
greed. the screens ripple with moths.

HOMAGE: WILLIAMS

what i am waiting for
is the opportunity to speak
about love

i am waiting for love!

tho no one tells you
there is no love
tho no one says
anything

i am going to
speak about love
to empty rooms
& the far crowded corners of
our witlessness
wild
        wild

listen this is a cry
not a poem
not a rock song
not even anything
i would look back at
not even what it
seems to be
a poem in the
shape of a voice

# HOSEKI

peonies in spheres, dock leaves
like claws, lambswort purple &
edible, a leggy girl in shorts,
drifting thru the garden, ask-
ing for her kids.
                it's seedy, late.
if i turn i'll see my father,
one foot on the runner of a
chrysler, 1934, his fierce face
mirrored in the door. *look,* i'll
say. a bird rocks in a pool, my
own kids scatter home-free,
                        blind
shadows on my hands & mouth so
i can't read, hoseki's "wither-
ing, art of the essential,"
stacked fossils.

# MEMORY OF ITALY

nightingales: we must have heard one
one spring morning, in the borghese,
hidden in the clusters of red trees
& stone, life laid out calm & lush,
the children home.
                              vishinsky, at the
UN, once told a hostile to come to
russia & hear them singing in the
south, in spring, by river & birch.
he would lose his politics & be
won over. or was it sickness to
be home?
                              i guessed that things seen
were beaten by things heard. i like
what you can grasp: bricks in the
field near paestum, salerno with its
tiled church, rowing at positano,
walking the night stone around the
campo, a picnic in the winter near
the empty walls of veio.
                                           here
the fog lifts & we see the crazy neon
of another indiana summer. a bird comes
easily, a cardinal by its throat.

## HOMAGE: QUASIMODO

in the dark the
enemy who is
coming has not
come yet

## 1963: A GIRL ABDUCTED

she combed her hair, kissed, stared
in the mirror, left the door wide &
was gone. *a blind ride, a bum steer.*
for half a year they looked for her,
in lakes parks drains motels & lots,
& found nothing. either she had been
neatly murdered or copped out, they
thought. but her mother said she was
the best girl in the world, a friend
that she went out with no one.
                    *plain
jane, & weird.* they probed some more,
& for a while everyone did. i remem-
ber a late afternoon on the berkeley
campus, a dumb kid idly poking gul-
lies, storm drains, under the big eu-
calyptus that we liked, scented with
rain & space & sea. it was a week be-
fore the death of kennedy.
                    all this
is in the papers, which still turn up
cliches for each calamity except our
walk. it seems now kennedy had to die
& that girl be spirited—is that the
word—away, & we think *no reason, no-
thing at all,* breathing eucalyptus in
the half dark, following her.

THREE FOR MY FATHER

*1*

behind your smile & your taut
child's face, i hear you tell
me how you made more extrac-
tions with your right hand
than any man in town.

                         father
power! you'd come to the door
& an ape would get out of the
chair, *doc you're a genius,*
who never heard his groans
under the mask.

                         laughing gas.
the wise guys from downtown
woke up clutching empty
mouths,

              tho i saw you drill
the desert where i sat, &
heard the pain they dream-
ed numb at the root, &
talk:

         *dead? alive? is dumb*
*pain sleep or sleep fear?*

*2*

remember the refugees you took
home during the war, seraphs
from dry heights, for whom i
did my thing, explained the
downtown map, & wore a but-
ton, *To Hell With Hitler,* who
finally went?

       & rabbi roehm,
who wasn't kind or unkind but
smelled of honeycake & bees
on the brain, & held the wine
we brought him in papery fin-
gers, & shook, & drank?

           that
year we fought in a dirt road
& you cracked my nose against
some insult to your light.

         rabbi,
blind crow on god's shoulder,
say i made a stone no one
would bite.

*3*

tell me the story of your life
again, you & the bear, wasting
its time at a streamhead, among
berries & burrs. it looks up,
sees you charge, enraged,
nose wide.
       you said you put a
hand down its throat, & turned
it inside out, & sent it spin-
ning, mucus coat, into the sky,
where it still goes.
          does it now?
who was the dreamer, who the
bear?

FOR MY FATHER IN FLORIDA

it was a fabulous scene for us, when you
sailed out in the middle of a hurricane
to tie up the tomato plants, like fdr,
since everything you nourished had to
grow. & there were other storms in ear-
ly fall, rolling branches, flooding
streets, & everyone going about their
business just the same.
                       now you live where
hurricanes are born, & i'm inland, &
have got to know tornadoes, how they
threaten a field or bash a road, sul-
len, sporadic, magnificent, nothing
to crow;
           & i can hear my own kids on
hot september nights, daddy what now,
& want to say, despite despite, my
father's work, & nothing to fear
but love itself.

## FOR MY FATHER

in places at the edge of a jaw or
shoulder, pink nipples, warts &
tubes:
             the patchwork of my father's
flesh, burnt cirques where the
grass never penetrates or heals,

                                      a
second growth. once a surgeon
caught one before it ruined you.
you came home ash faced, almost
picked off,
             & i was scared, tho now
you say you're not. what should
i do?


                    •


a wheel spinning into dark
flattens at both ends, go-
es square, brings nothing
but shape & shape, & never
stops stopping, more & more
as it nears nothing less.


                    •


*who am i to live so long? my
father died at 58,* you said.

WEATHER

wind runs & clashes at the
house all night. in the morn-
ing it has dropped the bird
feeder to one side, narrowed
the bread left out to tiny
cakes, hollowed the body
molds the kids made in the
snow & called angels. i put
my fist to the window above
their names & thumbs in
breath, & feel the cold a-
gainst the panes, the dry
air between.
            later, someone
wants us out, & we go to a
house where anyone can ask,
"now if my son was going
to be a poet, what would i
tell him?" tell him nothing,
idiot, i say slowly to my-
self, & then think better
of it, driving home, trees
shining & flashing, tell
him nothing if you know
what nothing is.

FOR RACHEL

anger what good
the flower is angrier than i am
so is the blood
that rights & jerks in the ground
when i slice it with my rake
my daughter following
pulling crocus flowers
off the flagstones where the sudden freeze
left them

## FOR JULIE

she's playing the same thing for
the fifth time today, cartwheels,
eggshells, a wolf is at the door.
she curls her fingers toward small
skills. she'll get there soon.
we all will.
                 so what else is new?
i want to throw her to the ceiling
again, & i hear the juncos in the
bush that holds its leaves all win-
ter & lets down in spring,
                            their
pellets in a thin vibrato, *fine
you are.*

## ANYTHING YOU WANT

*the eaters of men are coming,* said the
book i'd bought her, *the black eaters
of men!* she read it over, chewing on
her hair. a boy fled island savages,
armed only with dog, knife from a tomb,
& chutzpah. *Call It Courage,* c. 1941:
be calm, go harrow hell.
                         archaic now,
taboo, i wanted to say, & some of my
best friends are cannibals, & no one's
escaped yet or chased us here, & some-
day you'll read *Jew Suss Meets Trader
Vic,*
    but that's fable too, like alice
on the dark side of the glass. we are
all goys in pago pago.

## CH'AD G'AD YAW

*watch it,* i tell the kids, meaning
*stop look & listen,* & hammer in the
storms, crushing dry spiders & burnt
moths (one fell on the floor last
night & went under the couch, away
from the light).
           things pause, just
grackles checking trees, & we sleep
in a blind calm, until someone's at
the bed, *can i get in, bad dream,* &
breathes against an angel outside
swatting leaves.
              *take a load off
your cells,* i say, & hear my grand-
mother's, *the old get dark & go
down,* until we grew frightened
of her, & left.

# FRIDAY NIGHTS

she parceled out the flames, one for
each tip, & then three heads, which
could eat wood, but only fingered
the corner mirror, the stair;

                           & put
her face in her hands, & asked more
crumbs of daily breath, less quarrel-
ing from us, leprosy for hitler, i
never knew.

              i remember the candles
giving up body without absence,
their light from week to week
climbing our petty drifts,

                     to thank
god. it was so simple.

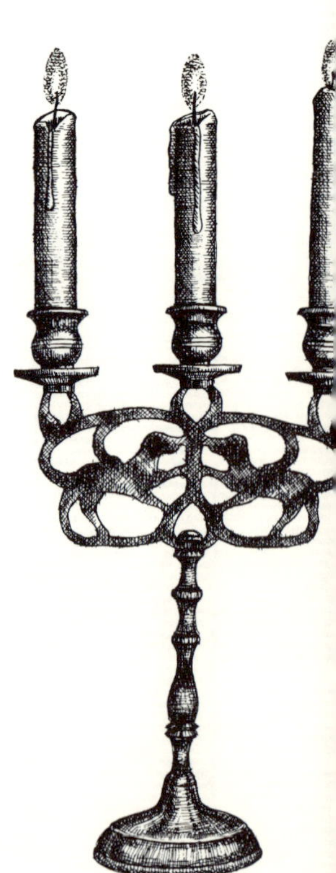

1913

& my father's grandfather
sat in a small room
playing shepherd's songs on a flute
& saying, over & over,
there will be a great war
there will be a great war

a fine tall blond-headed man
everyone looked at when he walked
a learned man a scholar

there will be a great war

# WAR POEM, 1968

wall of remote
heights & bends
of listless fields

turn savagely
to the river
where the trees

snap in the snow
a bird watches
the frozen mice

deer
i am sick
of talking about

vietnam:
these bridges
stringent iron

under which
the prints
of huge birds

that flew off
in september
following

the riverchain
to return as
blackbirds

stunning the trees
incredible demons
voyages

i am your mind
frozen but
the smallest



bloom may rouse

SOLDIERS ON A FERRY, 1941

they were singing around us,
all lifted face cap coat, as
if home could boom for half
a mile in the salty air, the
engine chugging clear.
                              "isn't
it too bad," harriet said. the
landing boards slopped, the
chains swung.
                    *Down by the Old,*
they started, one by one.

# SEPTEMBER

my long snub fingers type
continuously. when they
stop, i look out, at the
cracked birdbath near the
garage, the wild path thru
shabby scrub that never
evens out. tho it might
rain, a band begins, a tuba
farts, a bass drum knocks
dead on. i think of statues
in italian parks, hands
lopped, wrists all sutures,
joints. last night one
child couldn't sleep, &
wanted love before we left
(arms up, an old time hug);
as she moves toward her
fear she gets more real for
us. the other, all joy so
far, has nightmares; i
do too. one already here.

# INTERVAL

it's two weeks since no one
imagined a death, & i still
see the crumpled pamphlet
prayers, the candle in its
red glass, the florida heat
inert with leisure, damp.
here the alleys are all iris,
weeds choking gravel, vio-
lets rimming cans. in the
house we wash the stems,
breathe fresh earth, begin.

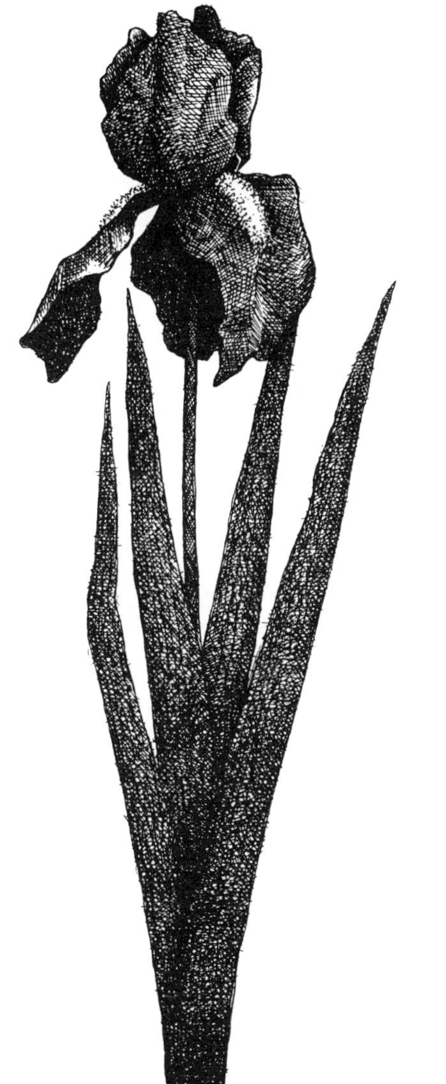

1972

summer, & i see ads for kids
pressed in ghettos (the word
is love), & want to waste no-
thing, like the skinny cat i
feed who goes after birds no
matter, & now & then tips one
& drops it, under the maples,
out back (what's the good)? &
what is the good? it's summer
on my swollen head, my thick
hands, the stiff-lipped dumb
who stomp around my tongue or
starve or sit on washer tops
in seconds stores, dealing
frigidaires, the wallace but-
tons sticking from their necks
(you hippie jew, you nigga lov-
in' fag, i'll kiss you on my
mouth if you don't buy it) &
we walk out. i work for power.
yevtushenko said it on tv the
other night, before a ghetto
black, "my poem is a mailed
fist," & made it sound decis-
ive for a minute, tho i know
better, both about poems & a-
bout yevtushenko (who buys?
who kills? who dies?)  the pow-
er i work for flickers in &
out, & will not be abused, excis-
ed, & goes its own way to its
own green hell the hell i say.

COUNTRY JOURNAL

*1*

early evening.
i am straining hard to do what i cannot
do well, read, think, print. outside
just as the dark comes, i see an owl
fleshed across the unmentionable.

                          in
the back a porcupine bobs across the
grass toward the shed, to chew man-
handled wood all night, herding its
two young. we light the jerky lamps.
at first the kerosene flames up, prints
the ceiling paw black.
                 later, after i
turn them out, in the afterglow, i watch
the blue filaments pinwheel & hiss. total
black.

*2*

i am still my own enemy, & feel it beat
around the house all night like a vamp,
sheltering me. it breaks into the covers,
touches your familiar humps in sheets. i
break out in a sudden twilight fear.
nothing is ordered.
                later an owl wakes me
with a child's long cry that starts me in
a dream like a tongue on my ear, & ends as
i come alive in a start of breath.
                    toward
light i think there is nothing here but me
& miracle. i come out of my socket, sleep
again. the children begin to chatter, & we
dress them, send them in the fleshed light
out for blueberries, which lie in the cereal
pale blue pale.

*3*

day after day here, i sit in the bedroom
study tight with boredom, "working on a
book." when i think i finish it i feel
released. under the stairs a heart ties
me with terror coming closer.

                                you fill
the downstairs rooms with flowers we
find in the meadows & woods like flags:
daisies, huge swollen pubises of eyes,
orange darting tongues, spear swells,
green thighs, stars that tip & split.
                                         i

go with you in a canoe to a part of the
pond we never saw, a spoon-shaped end with
enormous lily pads, a frog on one two hands
long, marsh grass that holds the bottom &
sucks the boat across. we talk lumpily &
see everything detail itself against us.

a night later, sleeping downstairs, i hear
the porcupine at its nightly work, gnawing
the legs of the porch. the trees drip gum
tick tick
                sugar maples hemlock iron scrub
pine blind walls alive with damp, light,
dry dirt, elephant hides.
                      i feel a groove
gum-thick & open my mouth to move it out.
it saws.

*4*

for two months time broils slowly,
into a fat no one will touch until
i take it off. slowly i build my
spirit like a lamp, with the por-
cupine, the garbage fixed raccoons,
the dog from the farm down-hill,
nose high with quills, a fox, a
cat. the trees whip huge balloons.

i keep stiff. i feel things change:
the girls move outside more freely
now; you are less restless than a
butterfly; i learn how to stand in
a space with trees drying & falling
around me; i watch the mice that
stay in the walls all winter. i am
in patience suddenly with death.

THREE MARRIAGE POEMS

*1963*

we took tomatoes, wine & bread, &
watched the seals, fat fingers on
the rocks, asleep from storm or
fin. butterflies, sky, wind flared
at the sea,
            the year we walked
its plate, point reyes, & let it
daze us. once you cried. to be
somewhere with someone else? no,
but you weren't good enough.
                                for
what? to break, heal, hate across
that space & light?
                    *breathe deep,*
they said before the gas. *it
cleans. it disinfects.*

*1970*

outside, the spring ghosts press
& flick. inside, you play handel,
the harmonious blacksmith, pre-
cise stroke & battering sandal.
                       you're
grey-eyed, clear as your father,
& the staring family in his photo,
who almost left bialystok in 1939:
                            a

town on a river bend, still there,
no one alive we'd know. it means
a bagel, transport, pits,
                   a stone
against the noises at the window,
& in first sleep, our kids.

*1975*

downstairs, the cello sounds un-
certain, furry as a rugstain, al-
ways underfoot.
                        you say you began
too late to make it grin & bow,
that it's still art, not felt,
                                        while
the puppy tears its rawhide like
the last chew in the world, the
kids come in & growl,
                        *dark, less,*
*enough.* wherever we're going,
we're there now.

## APROPOS

do you remember the dark shack we
rented, where it rained for weeks,
& nothing dried, & thumblong slugs
appeared one night—i crushed one
with a broom handle & swept the oth-
ers out. we hung a blanket & slept
half in shock, the kids in back. &
what love. the rain, the sea had
made you lovely, fleshy, quick. i
rubbed & blundered thru you; day
felt like a joke.
    *here be dragons,*
*at the end of summer,* i thought, &
could not get enough. then the sun
came back, & trouble.
      i remember. i
folded like the two halves of a
wound around a pearl. i don't ex-
aggerate. i kept it close, i keep
it now.

## ALL THAT, SO SIMPLE

that was the year we couldn't sleep.
by day the darkness held. we met &
wouldn't speak. there was nothing
for it but to stay in one place,
                              dark
going into trees, wind moving east,
years, all that, so simple. & never
guessed it would come back, & stand
here now, pawing the rug, almost
a guest.
              no one would believe. we
look outside & hold it to ourselves.

# THE REVOLUTION
# IS ACCOMPLISHED

it's done being cold, & a cold
wind leans thru the screens i
just put up, where the dog nos-
es to come in from the sun. be-
yond, the usual sparrows, a car-
dinal, a grackle's itchy croak.

                                       it's

common cold. in the yard things
stiffen for the jerk out of the
ground: the slabbed grass glows,
lanes are toenail blunt with
scrub. when the dog wants out a-
gain, i follow, into the wild
light, among cliches: i've piss-
ed away a month, need a poem,
endless life love luck,

                            points of
weather, flies to swallow, flat
mouth, dry tongue. when the
revolution is accomplished,
the old dog's done.

SUMMER TUNE

in the fishpond of
our landlady who
has emphysema, in-
cipient angina, a
dead husband who
ignored her, etc.
frogs pulse & bong.
i stay upstairs,
slap flying ants,
& when the kids
fight bomb down &
calm them gently
as i can. the high
tide fills with
silver sprats; the
sun can blind; trees
pick at the wind &
hold it on its
nose. it's your
father's first
season alone. he
sleeps on the porch,
all screen & glass,
& tells us what
he hears in the
dark: wind, water,
dogs. we are, he
tells us, every-
thing he has.

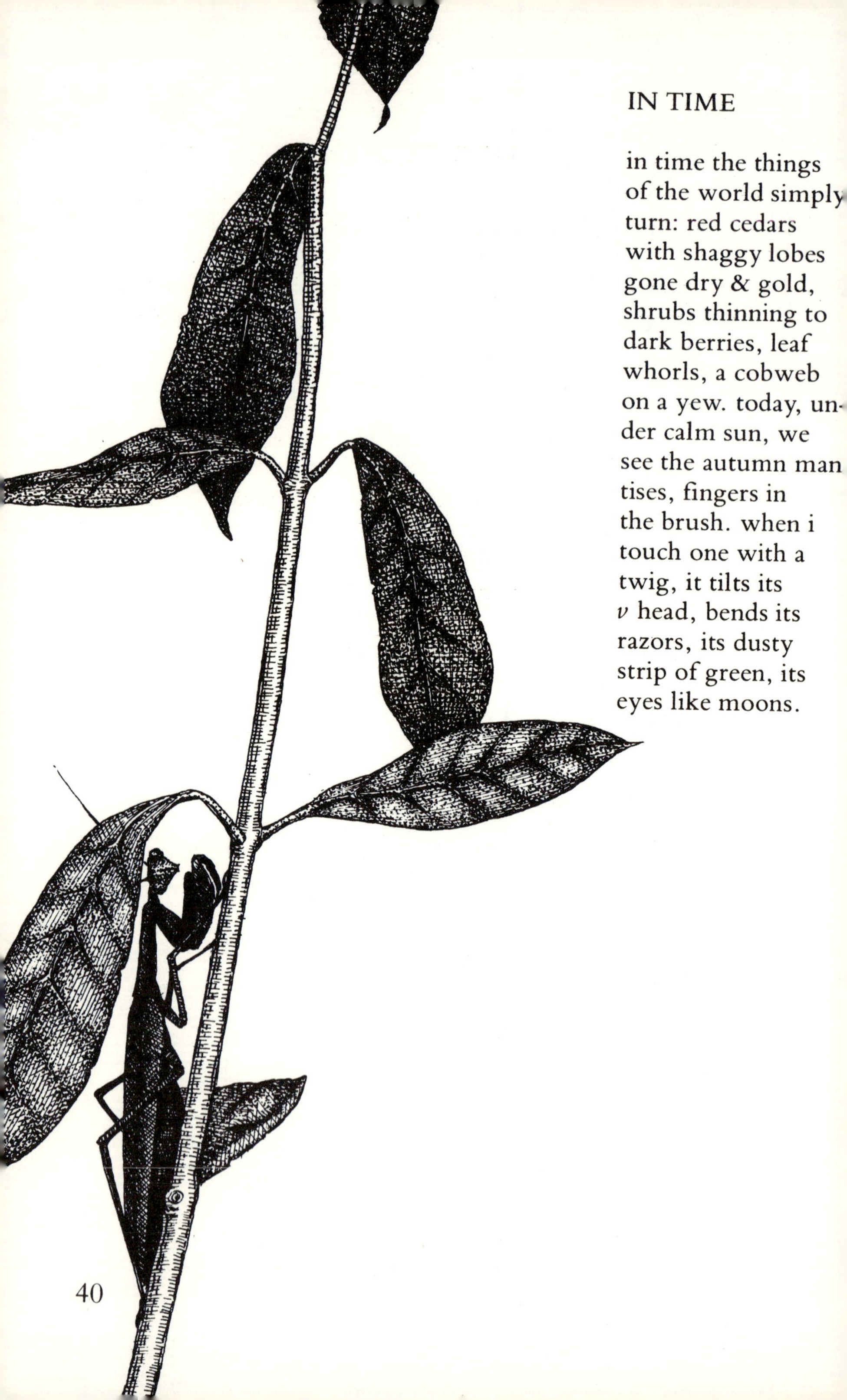

## IN TIME

in time the things
of the world simply
turn: red cedars
with shaggy lobes
gone dry & gold,
shrubs thinning to
dark berries, leaf
whorls, a cobweb
on a yew. today, un-
der calm sun, we
see the autumn man
tises, fingers in
the brush. when i
touch one with a
twig, it tilts its
*v* head, bends its
razors, its dusty
strip of green, its
eyes like moons.

## AUGUST, LATE

*There's a Fly in Here*

yesterday thru the basement window
i saw a daddy longlegs agst a screen
its light compass legs folded
& shafts of waxy leaves

now all that's secret is this fly
i don't know where it is
a minute back it was buzzing craftily
now it's just somewhere

this morning
the fly just came
& the daddy longlegs must have left

*The Air Is Doing Its Breathing*

the trees hold their leaves
like old men
they could be lame blind
or ashamed
so that standing under them
even before dark
we can hardly see

*Hanging Around*

just at midday the birds go
whieeper wheeper wheeper
the sky is dark
thunder comes bombing flat & fast

tho the rain doesn't come
everyone is waiting for everyone

*Hot*

out the window
a cat
its fur blinking
afternoon & sun
                    & i come
to whatever has been
weaving me up
                    & stand
rubbing my face

*Sudden Cold*

all day the wasps skim in
restless floaters     legs
dangling on gritty panels
screen & glass
                    drifting
to the attic     their anger
passing fear
                    *ash ash*

any day now
the silence will last

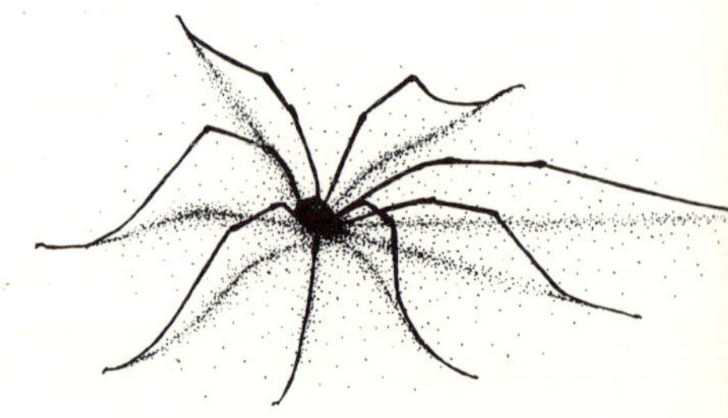

## A COUPLE OF DAYS

it's calm
& lovely

fog has spilled
milk on the trees

lower than 20°

brass rings on the belly
of an anaconda

.

doves walk
in the yard
in extra cold

under the feeder
on it
near the bushes

funky vultures
with small heads
steel pink


•


tonight
under the lamp
the rocks
my daughter put on my desk

a colorado one
a swiss one
blue white
sandy papery

"if you hold it in your hand maybe
you can see where you got it"

"i already did
it didn't work"


•

doves
pterodactyl shadows
in the old redbud

& a show of sparrows
in the tangled bush


•


in moments
of confusion
& rage

it helps
to complete a
sentence

like this
man is
an ocean

that can see
the ending of its
confusion & rage


•

the flow
of dazed sentences
hooked together the same
way & the final
blank
        the ending
that hadn't intend–
ed to go where it
went
        & the last
thing it wanted
to say which it
didn't
        & the
first
        all year the
compass swings like
a snowflake
                things
shine & stare

postcards
strasbourg a mile

out    its towers
radial in the

mist    dry
space on a road

grass pushed aside
sit eat

paté of goose
strong bread

one car goes by    the last
day of travel    or

sudden confusion here
immense chaos

of mist & light
then

pouring of music    birds
at the feeder

flocking toward
the grain i left


dove flying over snow

fat puff
turns fan

FIELD

one would take from it
old names of weeds,
the dripping faucet
that keeps birds near,
& buzzard-headed flies
& backs of snails.
                              ask
it to tap a finger,
raise a lid,
hear
its nothing doing
go ahead.

WRAP UP

the october evening's warm & dry,
& one cold spell will blow it in
a snap. i watch a window spider
trap moths by my light, & pull
them to the sill & into bags. it's
weird, like the news, all war from
xut to yak, & the anchorman's noise-
less patient eye, that holds the
global village in a net, & asks
who cares if no one dines, or cares
too much (i do, i don't).    the
moon is in the branches like a drunk.
a star blooms when i cut the set.

## FOR SU TUNG-P'O

a day breathes thru an end, another one,
all dark, which says i am
one better, tho it coughs up clouds
like liquid, fat curled leaves, dead
pears, a redbud turned all skeleton, &
things less sentimental, a constant knock
on feet of rakes & saws & bells
that claim our sleep.
                          i think, to clear
my head, of intelligent chinese, & then
i see them, watching boats on huge rivers,
drawing from mountains, trees, feeling
tall, altho they may be just two hands, a
head, some feet. one rubs a pool
of ink, smutches paper, writes characters,
links all to each, & drinks all night,
hilarious, without addiction. one praises
the moon, & speaks carelessly of exile.

WINTER PIECE

the small pot
hung between the
windows
keeps producing
small
pink flowers
incessant. i
who moved it
there
& wondered
what it would do
keep wondering.
water
is enough. a
bit
of earth.
heights of small
leaves. flow-
ers incessant.

## STARLING

tree to

tree pure
shadow in

the light
ning of a

leafless
branch

Photo by Natalie Leimkuhler

A native of New Jersey and a graduate of the University of Wisconsin and Harvard University, Neil Myers has taught creative writing and modern poetry at Purdue University since 1961. A former co-editor of *The Minnesota Review,* his poems have appeared widely in such publications as *The Massachusetts Review, The New York Times, Caterpillar, Esquire, Mademoiselle,* and elsewhere. His short collection of poems, *Tippecanoe,* with drawings by Tony Vevers, was published in 1972.

Neil Myers' poetry reflects his interest in the moods of local landscapes and in the language of ordinary experience. He writes of his work: "I'm not concerned with labels. I like poems that show energy and clarity, that deal with inward value held up against the weather, that are part of a constant process of making up one's mind about the world."

Donald K. Carter, graphic designer for the Purdue University Press, designed and illustrated *All That, So Simple.* Typographic Service of Indianapolis, Indiana, phototypeset the book in Bembo typefaces, and Thomson-Shore of Dexter, Michigan, printed it. The text stock is Beckett seventy-pound white laid and the cover stock is eighty-pound Curtis colophon white.